SHAKESPEARE:
KING LEAR

by
NICHOLAS BROOKE

*Professor of English Literature,
University of East Anglia*

EDWARD ARNOLD

© NICHOLAS BROOKE 1963

First published 1963 by
Edward Arnold (Publishers) Ltd.,
41 Bedford Square, London WC1B 3DQ

Reprinted 1964, 1967, 1969, 1971, 1973, 1975, 1977, 1979

ISBN: 0 7131 5081 5

Printed and bound in Great Britain at
The Camelot Press Ltd, Southampton

General Preface

The object of this series is to provide studies of individual novels, plays and groups of poems and essays which are known to be widely read by students. The emphasis is on clarification and evaluation; biographical and historical facts, while they may be discussed when they throw light on particular elements in a writer's work, are generally subordinated to critical discussion. What kind of work is this? What exactly goes on here? How good is this work, and why? These are the questions that each writer will try to answer.

It should be emphasized that these studies are written on the assumption that the reader has already read carefully the work discussed. The objective is not to enable students to deliver opinions about works they have not read, nor is it to provide ready-made ideas to be applied to works that have been read. In one sense all critical interpretation can be regarded as foisting opinions on readers, but to accept this is to deny the advantages of any sort of critical discussion directed at students or indeed at anybody else. The aim of these studies is to provide what Coleridge called in another context 'aids to reflection' about the works discussed. The interpretations are offered as suggestive rather than as definitive, in the hope of stimulating the reader into developing further his own insights. This is after all the function of all critical discourse among sensible people.

Because of the interest which this kind of study has aroused, it has been decided to extend it first from merely English literature to include also some selected works of American literature and now further to include selected works in English by Commonwealth writers. The criterion will remain that the book studied is important in itself and is widely read by students.

DAVID DAICHES

To my Mother
in memory of my Father

Acknowledgements

I have made very full use of Kenneth Muir's edition of the play in the Arden Shakespeare, and all quotations are taken from that. I have not attempted to disentangle the sources of particular ideas about the play for special acknowledgement: the books I have found most valuable are recommended for further reading at the end.

The substance of this book derives from lectures given in the Durham Colleges over a period of years; I owe a great deal to students there, both for criticism and encouragement.

Contents

Prologue

Melodrama, Morality, and Naturalism

The inertia of traditional approval for Shakespeare's plays often allows them to seem more like contemporary drama than a less prejudiced view would suggest. From the later nineteenth century until quite recently, the generality of successful new plays presented apparently 'natural' characters performing supposedly 'natural' actions. *King Lear* was regularly revived throughout this time[1] (as throughout all times since its first performance in the years 1604-6), although by that expectation it should have looked a very strange play indeed. Reduced to the bare bones of a summary, its actions seem crude, even absurd, its people sometimes very unnatural indeed. Lear's pride is not just humbled, it is reduced from supreme autocratic power to utter penury and insanity; his quarrel with Cordelia is resolved in abject contrition from him and unlimited charity from her; Goneril and Regan are not merely unkind, they are (both in cruelty and sensuality) forerunners of the Marquis de Sade; Edgar, exiled from his father's castle, chooses to live as a half-naked, half-witted beggar. All this suggests the extravagant implausibility of melodrama; and simultaneously the ease with which we can pin labels on to most of these characters (except Lear himself) as 'good' or 'evil' suggests a legacy from the tradition of morality plays which dominated the English stage for a hundred years before Shakespeare and his contemporaries created new worlds of theatrical possibility.

Such a play, one would think, should have been repugnant to an age which expected naturalism, when 'melodrama' and 'morality' were equally terms of abuse in the jargon of dramatic criticism. Yet the play's clearly defined physical and moral extremes do enable us to see directly what it is 'about': its scope is measured by the fullest possible range of human experience; and however 'unnatural' it may seem in one sense, it is in another sense just as an exploration of what is 'natural' that we have to regard it. It is easy to see that the heightening effect of performing on a

[1] although Lamb's conclusion that it was unactable was often remembered, and Bradley stated that it was 'the least often presented on the stage [of the major Tragedies], and the least successful there'.

stage makes such a representation possible; but it is much more difficult to recognise the means by which Shakespeare invests such a skeleton with the flesh of particular life, so that the play seems, at almost any given moment, to possess just that immediate sense of naturalism which, regarded overall, one might expect it to lack. In this respect, *Lear* resembles Shakespeare's last plays, whose plots if merely read, or reflected on outside the theatre, seem merely absurd; but which in actual perform-ance often seem utterly convincing, in the naturalness with which speech responds to situation. In the last plays, but not in *Lear*, one may some-times feel the impudence of sheer technical accomplishment in making the unnatural seem natural. The trick partly depends, I suspect, on the fact that we do not have to be so interested in just what leads up to a particular situation as Ibsen or Freud (or Bradley) were, provided that we feel the reality of human behaviour in the situation itself. So, for instance, we are not really much bothered about how Leontes, in *The Winter's Tale*, came to be jealous, but strongly aware of the fullness and complexity of the experience of sexual jealousy in his words. Samuel Johnson provided a useful diagnosis of this tendency in Shakespeare's work: 'the event which he represents will not happen, but if it were possible, its effects would probably be such as he has assigned.'[1] If we understand 'effects' here to mean, not so much 'what happens next', as all that properly belongs to the event, then this becomes immediately helpful in grasping the quality of *King Lear*. In the enormous feat of compression needed to encompass such a range in the two (or three) hours' traffic of the stage, it frequently seems to neglect a careful develop-ment of cause and effect in favour of a single concentration on particular 'effects', leaving causes to be only generally understood. Thus, for instance, we have really no clear idea in Act IV, scene vii how Lear comes to be waking in Cordelia's arms, but as the painful bareness of his utter-ance is met by the impulsive (and untruthful) reassurance of hers, all question of how this comes to be so is lost in the assurance that it *is* so:

> I know you do not love me; for your sisters
> Have, as I do remember, done me wrong:
> You have some cause, they have not.

Cor.   No cause, no cause. (73-75)

[1] *Preface to Shakespeare.*

The experience is radically different, but no less convincing, when in
V. iii Lear enters with Cordelia dead in his arms, roaring:

> Howl, howl, howl! O! you are men of stones:
> Had I your tongues and eyes, I'd use them so
> That heaven's vault should crack. (257-9)

The point can be extended through all the variety of the play: the complacent splendours of Lear's ceremonial speech in Act I; or the magni-
ficent rant with which he confronts the storm in Act III; or the bare
repetition of 'Then, kill, kill, kill, kill, kill, kill' which concludes his
revulsion against all physical life in IV. vi—and so on.

Poetic Speech

In stressing the absolute naturalness of these effects, I must push the
diagnosis a stage further here. These contrasting speeches are only *seemingly* natural: they are not the language any man would actually use;
if for no other reason, because they are in verse. Passionate speech tends
always to acquire its own rhythm; but verse is the completion of that
tendency. Not the forcing of speech into unnatural metre, but the fulfil-
ment of a naturally rhythmic utterance, and thus *more* 'natural' than any
actual man ever is. The rhythms in *Lear* are varied through as great a
range as the experience, and in this sense the use of verse becomes an
essential economy: it establishes both more fully, and more immediately,
the quality of each experience. I have already quoted from Lear's speech
in IV. vii; its extreme quietude and light continuity of rhythm are in
total contrast to the shattered tension of his madness in the previous
scene:

> What was thy cause?
> Adultery?
> Thou shalt not die: die for adultery! No:
> The wren goes to't, and the small gilded fly
> Does lecher in my sight.
> Let copulation thrive . . . (112-17)

Throughout that speech, as in the line and a half about the wren and the
fly, a rhetorical rhythm seems about to take charge; but it is always
frustrated by the exclamations which are finally all that is left:

> there's hell, there's darkness,
> There is the sulphurous pit—burning, scalding,
> Stench, consumption; fie, fie, fie! pah, pah! (129-31)

This broken fury is quite different from the sustained rhetoric with which Lear first opposed the storm:

> Blow, winds, and crack your cheeks! rage! blow!
> You cataracts and hurricanoes, spout
> Till you have drench'd our steeples, drown'd the cocks!
> You sulph'rous and thought-executing fires,
> Vaunt-couriers of oak-cleaving thunderbolts,
> Singe my white head! And thou, all-shaking thunder,
> Strike flat the thick rotundity o' th' world!
> Crack Nature's moulds, all germens spill at once
> That makes ingrateful man! (III. ii. 1-9)

The quotation has to be long, because, despite the modern exclamation marks, the rhythm is uninterrupted through nine superb lines. It is briefly recalled, like a theme in music, at the beginning of IV. vii, as Cordelia nurses the sleeping King:

> Was this a face
> To be oppos'd against the warring winds?
> To stand against the deep dread-bolted thunder?
> In the most terrible and nimble stroke
> Of quick, cross lightning? (31-35)

Cordelia, of course, contains the fury in a calmer tone; but her rhetorical phrases recapitulate the splendour that has been, in her word, 'untuned' in the jarring speeches of IV. vi; it is resolved in the utter contrast of the waking speech:

> Pray, do not mock me:
> I am a very foolish fond old man,
> Fourscore and upward, not an hour more or less;
> And, to deal plainly,
> I fear I am not in my perfect mind. (IV. vii. 59-63)

The unemphatic continuity of rhythm marks a restoration; but not, of

course, to anything like the same thing: there is no splendour here, and
no great assurance either.

It becomes clear that analysis of the verse of *Lear* would, if extended
over the whole play, reveal a musical kind of structure which, by virtue
of its range and magnitude, would have to be called symphonic. Such an
analysis is an essential part of commentary, because the verse is in no
possible sense a gratuitous addition—a superfluous 'beauty'—but, in its
varied tones relating, developing and contrasting with each other,
contributes very largely to our awareness of a comprehensive structure
of experience in the whole. Understanding this is one of the essential
routes to understanding the play. I have suggested by this means something of its range; but that has to be extended to include the easy informal
prose of the opening dialogue, or the complacent royalty of Lear's first
speeches, as well as the scherzo-like snatches of folk-song characteristic
of the Fool. This sense of a musical coherence is, of course, characteristic
of Shakespeare's plays from first to last; but *Lear*, it seems to me, stands
with *Antony and Cleopatra* as the supreme achievement in this kind.

Ideas and Images

Musical analogies, however revealing, are also misleading about
poetry, dramatic or otherwise. It is really only in rhythm that the resem-
blance is at all close; the aural properties of words, even the most ono-
matopoeic of them, are very slight compared to an orchestra of wind and
strings, and the 'themes' which recur in the rhythmic structure are not
so much sounds as ideas and images. Here, yet again, re-iteration of
words conveying similar senses insists on the range of the play's concerns:

> What can you say to draw
>   A third more opulent than your sisters? Speak.
> *Cor.* Nothing, my lord.
> *Lear.* Nothing?
> *Cor.* Nothing.
> *Lear.* Nothing will come of nothing: speak again. (I. i. 85-90)

In the simplest sense, 'Nothing' is only a reply to 'What can you say?';
but it is also in immediate contrast to Lear's word 'opulent' which sums
up his own utterance as well as Goneril's and Regan's; and Cordelia's
abruptness changes Lear's tone from 'The vines of France and milk of

Burgundy' to 'Nothing will come of nothing'. Repeated five times in scarcely two lines, 'nothing' becomes a key-word, and it recurs conspicuously during the rest of the Act. Opulence is equally prominent later in, for instance, the perverse luxury of which Lear accuses Regan in II. iv:

> Thou art a lady;
> If only to go warm were gorgeous,
> Why, nature needs not what thou gorgeous wear'st,
> Which scarcely keeps thee warm. (269-72)

'Nothing' is obviously an unspoken word here, and the contrast is complicated by a third term—'need'—which Lear suggests as governing proportion, what is neither superfluous nor inadequate; the idea of 'clothing' is involved equally in 'need' or 'opulence' and either of them contrasts with 'nature' as much as with 'nothing'. All these key-words centre here in the debate on 'nature', and man's place in it:

> our basest beggars
> Are in the poorest thing superfluous:
> Allow not nature more than nature needs,
> Man's life is cheap as beast's. (266-9)

Man, throughout the play, is continually compared to beasts, whether savage or merely inferior, like dogs; and beggary appears not only in the frequent use of the word, but also when Edgar takes on the rôle of beggar, and so makes the idea of inadequate clothing actually seen as well as heard. And when Lear, imagining beggars in the storm, speaks of their 'houseless heads and unfed sides', their 'loop'd and window'd raggedness', he associates clothing with another recurrent image, of housing, which may similarly be either necessary shelter or superfluous pomp.

Recurrent images, whether purely verbal or made actually visible on the stage, echo thus through the play, clustering associations of feelings and ideas in its development. The most obvious instance of all is the opposition of 'sight' to 'blindness', metaphorical when applied to Lear struggling with mental blindness, literal in the putting out of Gloucester's eyes. The idea of seeing, well or ill, has therefore a particular significance in both the relating and the distinguishing of the two plots. That they are alike is, if one regards only a summary, obvious: Lear's relations with his daughters, Gloucester's with his sons, are virtually the same; both suffer appallingly, are rendered homeless, and are finally restored to some degree of comfort by the children they have wronged, before they die. But though in summary they are alike, as we discover it in seeing the play the likeness emerges only along with our recognition of the differences. In fact, the differences are apparent first: Gloucester telling Kent about Edmund's conception, in light and witty prose, is a figure of very different weight from the Lear who shortly after speaks with full assurance of his royal authority. Such a difference remains, but it is not always so easy to feel: *readers* of the play may announce complacently that Gloucester's punishment, like his crime, is physical, whereas Lear's cracking mind is a far more terrible torment; *audiences* in the theatre will, I think, say the same, but with less complacence after their eyes have been forced to watch Gloucester's squirted out:

> Out, vile jelly!
> Where is thy lustre now? (III. vii. 82–83)

Only by enduring that can we begin to understand the suffering of Lear himself.

The Two Stories

No doubt in the primitive myths from which these stories grew, they were once identical; their difference in the play, Shakespeare develops from two quite different sources. The Lear story he took in many respects from an older play, *King Leir*; but these respects are more a matter of incident than interpretation; the old play offered a far more stupid and criminal King who is eventually forgiven and reconciled to Cordelia, who like himself is allowed to live. The story, in this form, has been adapted to the function of a crude moral fable; but Shakespeare reverted to the more primitive sense of it in the form in which it appears in the *Mirror for Magistrates*, Holinshed's *Chronicles*, and Spenser's *Faerie Queene* (Book 2, canto xi). In all these it retains the amoral savagery of folk tale, ending in Lear's death and Cordelia's suicide. Suicide, we may well feel, is not a possibility for Shakespeare's Cordelia, but her death at all seemed so shocking that it was not represented on the stage for more than a hundred years after Tate's version was produced in the Restoration theatre; and Dr. Johnson found it too painful an affront to our love of justice. Johnson's devotion to poetic justice is not a neo-classical irrelevance here: whatever wrongs are exchanged between Lear and Cordelia in Act I are fully atoned in Act IV, scene vii, from which I have quoted; yet an Act later Cordelia is gratuitously hanged, and Lear dies of a broken heart; in between, Edgar has commented to Edmund on their father:

> The Gods are just, and of our pleasant vices
> Make instruments to plague us;
> The dark and vicious place where thee he got
> Cost him his eyes. (V. iii. 170–3)

It is plainly impossible to father this idea on Shakespeare, as a conception of justice which costs Cordelia her life. But Edgar's 'sentence' is still in our ears when we see Cordelia die of an instrument no gods made out of her vices, pleasant or otherwise. In other words, the juxtaposition of the two plots directly confronts the idea of justice with that of wild injustice, and poetic justice is confined to the sub-plot. The Gloucester story Shakespeare took from Sidney's *Arcadia*, where it appears characteristically as a sophisticated, moralised version of the Lear myth. A Paphlagonian king is brought to repentance by the kindness of his good legitimate son, after the wickedness of his concubine's offspring had tempted him to cruelty. 'Poetic justice' is precisely what Sidney was concerned to present: an offence against the sanctity of marriage (more offensive in detail than Gloucester's is made to seem) brings its *due* punishment.

In short, Shakespeare selects from his sources two radically different versions of the same story: an amoral tale of savagery and death, and a highly moral one of crime and punishment. Their juxtaposition challenges our belief in ultimate justice; and, it can be noted at once, it is the moral story of Gloucester and his sons which we have seen to be offered as the more superficial of the two.

Five Acts

It was claimed, at the beginning of this chapter, that *King Lear* depends for its success as a play on the character of its verse; that, in other words, it is essentially poetic drama, and not simply a play in verse. Subsequent discussion of the implications of the poetry could seem rather to wander into viewing it as a dramatic poem. The stress must finally be reversed: bird's-eye views of any literature are misleading; of a play particularly so. The poetry here is encountered by an audience as the speech of living men and women on the stage; any sense of unity, in verse, imagery, plot alike can only grow out of that. And in the theatre, even more than in reading, our attention is absorbed at any moment in the current scene. The experience of the play, the sense of its significance, develops in the sequence of events; and to deprive the events of that sequence and to discuss them as if they were simultaneous, is to falsify the nature of drama, and lose the vital impact of each new event on its predecessor. In the case of *King Lear* it seems to me that the five Acts into which the early editions divided the play do correspond to its actual organisation (whether Shakespeare envisaged intervals or not). Act I carries Lear from despotism to his first rebuff; Act II proceeds to his total exclusion from shelter and company; Act III exposes him to the extreme elements and cracks his mind, while Gloucester has his eyes put out; Act IV seems to lead them both towards reconciliation and peace; and Act V reverses that movement towards hope in final defeat and death. I propose, therefore, to observe these units in trying to develop a discussion of the play towards some grasp (it can never be more than partial) of its significance. There is no intention of providing a pedestrian scene by scene commentary, and the amount of space given to each Act is not in proportion to its importance, but simply governed by convenience. The sub-headings are intended to mark my progress through the play, rather than to provide a detailed summary of its structure.

B

Act I: Royal Lear

It is still not uncommon to read accounts of *King Lear* which offer Lear's wilful folly in I. i as the fault which brings the vengeful heavens literally crashing about him; and this view of the play has been, occasionally, extended to represent Cordelia's obstinancy here as a crime for which she, too, must ultimately die. Times change, of course; Victorian fathers would not have liked to be told:

> I love your Majesty
> According to my bond; no more nor less. (92-93)

and they might, like Lear, have retorted:

> Let pride, which she calls plainness, marry her. (129)

But no competent audience can fail to note that Cordelia is right, Lear wrong; though it does Shakespeare's dramatic power less than justice to think of Cordelia as *wholly* right, Lear *wholly* wrong. His senile absurdity jars on her nerves, and the abruptness of her 'Nothing' comes partly from exacerbation. She is right, of course; but she is also rude. She challenges Lear's temper, and the rest follows. It follows, but it has not the remotest connection with justice, to either of them. Justice, in any sense, can require no more than the perfect contrition and forgiveness seen in IV. vii; but that is not the end of the play.

No more is this first scene the end of Act I, which includes Edmund's self-declarations, brings Lear's and Edgar's rejections to a similar point, and has its own decisive conclusion in the first Lear-Fool scene, the first hints both of insight and insanity: 'I did her wrong' and 'O! let me not be mad, not mad, sweet heaven'. The distinction I am trying to enforce is one of weight, or perspective: the first scene is rather a prologue than an Act; or to put it another way, it provides the data from which the play develops, not the major crimes on which the tragedy depends (which are, in fact, committed in Acts II and III). It directs our attention forwards into what follows, not backwards into quaint speculation as to why Lear prepares a division of his kingdom into three *equal* parts, and then holds a competition to decide who gets the largest. Of course that is silly, regarded as dramatic action; but it is not dramatic in that sense, it is a ritual of the royal prerogative. And as a ritual, it is no sillier than most—for instance the official 'Opening' of a building that has been in full use for months or years.

Ritual into Drama: Lear and Cordelia (I. i. 1-119)

Our sense of this as ritual is enforced by the extreme contrast with the light, informal prose conversation which precedes it: Kent and Gloucester chatting bawdily about Edmund's birth are interrupted by the royal procession, and Lear's ceremonial utterance:

> Meantime, we shall express our darker purpose. (36)

This tone is sustained overall for fifty lines, but there are more ominous, and sensitive, implications as well:

> and 'tis our fast intent
> To shake all cares and business from our age,
> Conferring them on younger strengths, while we
> Unburthen'd crawl toward death. (38-41)

The contrasts of age-youth, care-ease, are given full weight; but they carry over into a less simple sense in the last line: 'crawl' is the action of the *over*-burdened, the exhausted animal; a private, not a ceremonial experience. It is some while before Lear touches that note again, but our sense of it is sustained in Cordelia's asides to her sisters' speeches. The incompleteness of ritual is fully pointed.

The spacious royal rhythm, carrying imagery of rich and fertile nature, expands through the confident amplitude of:

> Of all these bounds, even from this line to this,
> With shadowy forests and with champains rich'd,
> With plenteous rivers and wide-skirted meads,
> We make thee lady. (63-66)

This reaches its climax in Lear's invitation to Cordelia to draw a third more opulent than her sisters, when it is shattered by her 'Nothing, my lord'. The contrast is enormous, and on every level: the opulence of rhythm is jarred by staccato brevity; the fertility of rich champains, vines and milk is reduced to 'Nothing will come of nothing'; and the opulent assurance of public ritual is abruptly translated into drama—the personal conflict of Lear and Cordelia, which I described as a mutual exacerbation of nerves. Against the not-too-sweet reasonableness of Cordelia's distribution of her affection between husband and father, and Kent's support for her, Lear develops a new verse, the splendour of anger:

> Peace, Kent!
> Come not between the Dragon and his wrath. (121-2)

This is no longer the royal ritual, but the royal nature itself. The movement through this scene is very rapid, but supported by the contrasting tones of the verse, and the brief but telling effect of living human relationships, it is merely perverse to call it unconvincing. And worse still when actors, as some do, try to contain all this within the 'character' of a senile fool. A bleating Lear is fatal to the scene: he is here (what he calls himself later when the truth has gone) 'every inch a King', who justifies Kent's address:

> Royal Lear,
> Whom I have ever honour'd as my King. (139-40)

Instinct and Reason: Lear and Kent (I. i. 120-282)

But the greatness that is royal authority, is also in the wrong; and, pursuing its wrongness, approaches an opposite state. The feeling of Lear's age so far has been, so much the more a King; the opposite ('Unburthen'd crawl toward death') returns with Kent's

> be Kent unmannerly,
> When Lear is mad. What would'st thou do, old man? (145-6)

Kent stands between the dragon and his wrath, and the reduction of greatness to mere 'old man' is made via the charge of madness. Lear's full journey from Royal Dragon to bare forked animal via total disruption of mind is anticipated; and the key-terms are established:

Lear.	Out of my sight!
Kent.	See better, Lear; and let me still remain
	The true blank of thine eye. (157-9)

Madness is identified as distorted vision, not seeing things as they are. Lear in his rage invokes divine aid:

Lear.	Now, by Apollo,—
Kent.	Now, by Apollo, King,
	Thou swear'st thy Gods in vain. (160-1)

Kent's 'thy Gods' seems almost to suggest a Christian rebuking a pagan; in fact, Kent himself invokes the gods shortly afterwards, but this stress does establish the pagan world in which the play is set. Shakespeare is far more careful here than elsewhere to avoid even casual reference to the Christian God, so that the 'argument' of the play is firmly placed in a natural world, with no appeal available to dogmatic 'truths'. Hence, however strongly Christian overtones may occasionally be heard, they are established here by direct exploration of nature itself, and not by assumption from tradition or the New Testament.

This emphasises that the clash between Lear and Kent is already one between different concepts of 'nature'. Both assume an ultimate sense of order; but where for Lear this is a matter of hierarchy and unquestioned power, for Kent it depends on reason. Lear's order is, by contrast, unreasonable; the Dragon's power is instinctive:

> thou hast sought . . .
> To come betwixt our sentence and our power,
> Which nor our nature nor our place can bear,
> Our potency made good, take thy reward. (168-72)

The word 'potency' has worried editors: its force seems to me to define the relation of 'nature' and 'place'. Lear's 'power' is his position, 'made good' by his nature—his *instinct* of authority; but that is also, in Kent's words, 'hideous rashness'.

Such a nature is 'unredeemed', not so much because it is pagan, as because it is, for Lear, complete without submission to Reason. It stands outside the rationale of good sense to which both Cordelia and Kent appeal. Hence it is 'blind' as instinct is blind, where reasonableness is 'sight'. But this does not mean that Cordelia and Kent are rationalists: their 'nature', however reasonable, also has roots in instinct, seen in their stress on love. The connection is not an easy one, and Cordelia's

> That lord whose hand must take my plight shall carry
> Half my love with him, half my care and duty: (101-2)

seems clumsy in its alignment of affection and reason. A love so neatly divisible into halves is more rational than convincing. But the assurance of affection in Kent's

> The Gods to their dear shelter take thee, maid, (182)

is unmistakeable. Love becomes the theme of a long debate between Lear, Burgundy and France, with Cordelia as the object; and it is associated with her as a central value in the play.

Cold Calculation: Goneril and Regan (I. i. 283-308)

The tension of the scene relaxes in Cordelia's wooing, and it ends as it began, in plain prose. Goneril and Regan are eminently reasonable in their assessment of Lear's conduct:

Reg. 'Tis the infirmity of his age; yet he hath ever but slenderly known himself.
Gon. The best and soundest of his time hath been but rash; then must we look from his age, to receive not alone the imperfections of long-engraffed condition, but therewithal the unruly waywardness that infirm and choleric years bring with them. (293-9)

The peculiar quality of this is that they are right: they do see clearly. But this reasonableness is distinct from Kent's; devoid of affection, clarity of sight becomes coldness of calculation. Goneril's prose sounds like a scientific textbook (or one of Bacon's Essays), and its contrast with the poetries before stresses the absence here of any sense of the contrasting values that have been established.

Rational Control: Edmund (I. ii)

That completes the first scene, but not the first movement of the play. Two things remain to be established in the range of utterances and ideas:

Edmund's, and the Fool's. Edmund's soliloquy (ii. 1-22) is in verse, but quite unlike the verse of scene i, except when it verges on parody: 'Thou, Nature, art my goddess' may sound like Lear, but only in mockery. For the rest, Edmund's verse brings together the cynical wit of his father's prose with the calculating reason of Goneril's; it is, in fact, very close to prose, but developing the rhythmic impetus of a positive attitude. Edmund's goddess Nature is not Lear's or Kent's; it is in several senses 'base nature', bastard in its values. He plays persistently on two words, 'base' and 'legitimate'. Legitimacy is all law and order, which he stands outside. For him, 'love' is 'lusty stealth'; Lear's 'place and authority' is 'the plague of custom'; the family coherence of Cordelia's values is 'a dull, stale, tired bed'; and Kent's impersonal 'reason' becomes 'my invention'. If that thrive

> Edmund the base
> Shall top th' legitimate. (20-21)

In fact, Edmund's world is bare of values, as it is bare of all respect and of all gods. It works on simple laws, available to the manipulator. Edmund, like Bacon and his hero Machiavelli, studies 'what men do, and not what they ought to do', in order to bend the world to his own erect will. Edmund's scepticism disposes of all beliefs and all loyalties; it gives to his utterance a freedom of tone, springing from his self-sufficiency. This is far from the heroic self-assertion of Marlowe's heroes, but it has a freshness, and a sheer delight in his own activity, which makes it (here at least: he becomes less interesting later) an important addition to the ideas as well as to the characters of the play. His emergence here, after Goneril's and Regan's dialogue, has another significance. They have suggested, very reasonably, that what Lear lacks is self-control; once we have seen it in Edmund we cannot conceivably wish such control for Lear.

Nothing: Lear and the Fool (I. iv and v)

The last of the symphonic variations of tone is the most complete: to the Fool's utterance in scene iv. The Fool is fundamentally an anti-body, a complete contrast to everybody, as one feels in his bare prose, and in his verse, which is more unlike other poetries even than prose. In one sense, this is a form of parody, the serious themes seen as a joke; the Fool does make us laugh. But in another sense, it represents a kind of clarity; the Fool sees the issue in its bare essentials:

Kent. This is nothing, Fool.

Fool. Then 'tis like the breath of an unfee'd lawyer; you gave me nothing for't. Can you make no use of nothing, Nuncle?

Lear. Why, no, boy; nothing can be made out of nothing.

Fool. [*To Kent.*] Prithee, tell him, so much the rent of his land comes to: he will not believe a Fool. (134-41)

The echo of Lear's earlier 'Nothing will come of nothing' is striking, and so is the difference. That was verse, working in a context of poetry involving a complex sense of values; this is prose, a mere statement of fact shorn of all the previous overtones. And the Fool applies it to the most prosaic sense of value: 'so much the rent of his land comes to'. Strip the play of poetic visions, and you arrive at this: salutary common sense, which is also the negation of any real sense of value. Thus the Fool's jingle of proverbs (ll. 124-33) ends in nonsense; the logic of such common sense confounds itself, and ends in mere negation.

It is not surprising, then, that the Fool is melancholic. His verse is commonly snatches of folk-song, opposing joy and sorrow in a context of complete fatalism:

> Then they for sudden joy did weep,
>   And I for sorrow sung,
> That such a king should play bo-peep,
>   And go the fools among. (182-5)

At this level the Fool has his profoundest impact in the play. To this sense, the instinctive confidence in natural order which Lear manifests, or the moral effort of Cordelia and Kent, or the assertion of human will against an amoral universe which Edmund attempts, all are equally futile. The 'simplicity' of the Fool's verse can be seen as the simplicity of nature thought of as without any grand order, and without the least vestige of human pride; he does not question whether the pride is true or false, he simply omits it. Hence his speech is always melancholy, and fragmentary. This emerges in his relations with Lear, in the notorious fact that he offers to comfort but always succeeds in torturing; at first because he deflates false pride, ultimately because his negation is total.

We feel the contrast immediately Lear clashes with Goneril:

> O most small fault,
> How ugly didst thou in Cordelia show!
> Which, like an engine, wrench'd my frame of nature
> From the fix'd place, drew from my heart all love,
> And added to the gall. O Lear, Lear, Lear!
> Beat at this gate, that let thy folly in,
> And thy dear judgment out! (275-81)

Lear's 'frame of nature' asserts very positively an idea of order which includes a moral order. Hence it contrasts with the Fool's comment:

> The hedge-sparrow fed the cuckoo so long,
> That it's had it head bit off by it young. (224-5)

Nothing follows from such a statement; but for Lear the wrenched frame of external nature means a wrenching of his nature; madness 'beat at this gate'. His reaction is the roaring curse on Goneril:

> Hear, Nature, hear! dear Goddess, hear!
> Suspend thy purpose, if thou didst intend
> To make this creature fruitful!
> Into her womb convey sterility! (284-7)

This is rant—a wrenched frame indeed—but it is yet an utterance of a splendour distinctively Lear's. In calling on the 'dear Goddess' to provide an adequate punishment for Goneril, Lear restores his confidence in his dragon force, and in the frame of nature that such supernatural justice would affirm. But the confidence is incomplete; the speech *is* rant, and Lear returns to say:

> I am asham'd
> That thou hast power to shake my manhood thus; (305-6)

and so:

> Old fond eyes,
> Beweep this cause again, I'll pluck ye out. (310-11)

From this develops the last movement of Act I, the Fool's prose at its most trivial, witty jokes cracked at Lear's expense, while his 'old fond eyes' get new glimpses of the truth: 'I did her wrong', and so:

Fool. The reason why the seven stars are no mo than seven is a pretty
    reason.
Lear. Because they are not eight?
Fool. Yes, indeed: thou would'st make a good Fool. (v. 35-39)

The implication is that facts should be accepted as bare facts; but Lear
cannot forget his nature. He cannot remain a good Fool, but instead
exclaims:

> O! let me not be mad, not mad, sweet heaven;
> Keep me in temper; I would not be mad! (47-48)

That cadence virtually concludes Act I: in its deeply moving summary
of the personal experience, it simultaneously sums up the thematic
issues, the tension between a frame of nature in which man has the pride
of a moral place, and a framelessness in which moral action has no
significance, and pride is only delusion. In that case, two responses are
possible: one is the Fool's sad acceptance, the other Edmund's cold but
gay attempt at manipulation. Neither is within Lear's vision; for him
there is only a wrenched frame, and the threat of madness.

Act II: Reason not the Need

Deceptive Reason: Edmund (II. i)

Act I ends with Lear's first exit from a home, and from his frame of
nature. He is no longer Royal Lear, but still pursues the notion of being
an unburdened old man. Act II is given over to the furies, a remorseless
stripping from him of all his means of living, including finally the shelter
of any home at all. Superficially, Regan's repudiation simply echoes
Goneril's; in fact our sense of it is different, and much more fundamental.
Act I reached towards the fundamentals of human life in exploring moral
values in relation to the natural world; but the norms of moral judgement remained clear and available to guide us among the characters and
their acts. In Act II the challenge is carried to the basis of judgement itself.
In Act I we knew Lear's fault, Cordelia's honesty, Goneril's and Regan's

blatant hypocrisy, Edmund's dangerousness and Lear's pathetic (but still powerful) indignation. All these judgements are obvious, and available to any common sense, off or on the stage. But it would need much more than common sense for Gloucester in Act II to penetrate the deception practised on him, or even (if they cared to) for Regan and Cornwall either.

The deceptive evidences of affection in Goneril and Regan were 'asked for' by Lear's folly; Edmund's deception reaches a deeper level because it is not in that way asked for by any demand of Gloucester's. And what Edmund says is not nearly so transparent as the fulsome utterances of the sisters:

> But that I told him, the revenging Gods
> 'Gainst parricides did all the thunder bend;
> Spoke with how manifold and strong a bond
> The child was bound to th' father. (i. 45-8)

We can hear an echo here of Cordelia's 'According to my bond; no more nor less'; but the tone is not Cordelia's. Edmund's words move with a blatant rhetorical confidence; we, knowing the truth, can grasp the falsity exactly, but Gloucester has no chance of doing so.

Edmund, in fact, has precisely the Baconian power he wanted: he has gained control of nature, for he can manipulate Gloucester's affections which should be seated beyond the reach of another man's reason. In a sense they are beyond reason, but the sensory source of affection is absent, Gloucester does not *see* Edgar. It was, of course, an Elizabethan commonplace that reason should control affection, and that is here both demonstrated and abused. For Edmund, the superiority of reason is a matter of power; but what unsettles Gloucester is rational 'proof'. Reason thus becomes doubly questionable, both as capable of simulating affection, and as incapable of judging it.

Hence the deliberation with which, in the latter part of this Act, the orthodox relations of reason and affection are reversed: Goneril and Regan apply arguments far more seemingly reasonable than Edmund's; they may even be right; but when Lear finally bursts out 'O! reason not the need', it is not just our sympathy that is with him, it is our judgement too. Lear's unburdened old age is guilty of frivolity—so we are told; but just as Gloucester never sees Edgar, so we never see Lear's knights whose conduct is the source of argument.[1] In one sense, the evidence is against believing Regan's account of them:

Reg.	Was he not companion with the riotous knights
	That tended upon my father?
Glou.	I know not, Madam; 'tis too bad, too bad.
Edm.	Yes, Madam, he was of that consort. (i. 94-97)

Edmund's testimony is the opposite of convincing; Edgar may never have kept such company; or, their character may not in fact be 'riotous'. The only one we *see* is the disguised Kent confronting Oswald and being put in the stocks: his behaviour might be called riotous, but it is provoked.

But when Lear comes to judgement, he does not defend his followers, or their riots; he opposes Regan's 'reasonable' condemnation, not with evidence to the contrary, but simply with an oscillation between passionate anger and appeals to affection. In short, to grasp this scene, we must see that the case for Goneril and Regan may be perfectly reasonable; whatever the facts, this royal nature charging about unemployed with a hundred knights is likely, at the least, to prove a nuisance. Yet our judgement is wholly for Lear; our concern for facts and reason has been seriously weakened, and the dramatic force of the scene compels us to grasp affection instead. The affection that is in Lear; and the affection of Kent, Gloucester and (as Kent assures us) of Cordelia for Lear. And this again is manifest in Lear's utterance, as he reacts to the sight of Kent in the stocks and to Cornwall refusing to come forth:

> Are thee inform'd of this? My breath and blood!
> Fiery! the fiery Duke! Tell the hot Duke that—
> No, but not yet; may be he is not well:
> Infirmity doth still neglect all office
> Whereto our health is bound; we are not ourselves
> When Nature, being oppress'd, commands the mind
> To suffer with the body. I'll forbear;

[1] Peter Brook, in his justly celebrated Stratford production in 1962, brought them riotously on to the stage. In thus making it clear that Goneril and Regan have some show of right, he may have been justified; but it seems clear in the text that we should never actually *know* what their conduct was.

> And am fall'n out with my more headier will,
> To take the indispos'd and sickly fit
> For the sound man. Death on my state! wherefore
> Should he sit here? (iv. 103-13)

Both the instability and the vulnerability of affection are amply demonstrated here. The oscillations are only dubiously reasonable; but the will
to sustain affection, and the violence provoked by its violation, are
manifest. With every evidence of the unreliability of feelings, it is on
them that we base our judgement.

Interlude: Kent and Edgar (II. ii and iii)

That contrast, that disturbance of orthodox attitudes to reason and
affection, is achieved in the two main parts of the Act: Edmund's in
scene i, and Lear's in scene iv. Two further matters are developed in two
semi-choric soliloquies in the middle scenes, Kent's and Edgar's. Kent
indicates his presence in the stocks as an emblem of Lear's fallen greatness (the visual effects of the play are constantly referred to the imagery);
this is the bottom of Fortune's wheel. He goes on to hint that the wheel
will turn on, and gives here the first hint of Cordelia's intended invasion.
But the wheel of Fortune is an image of fate, not providence; and though
Kent offers hope for particular people, he sees none for the natural
order:

> All weary and o'erwatched,
> Take vantage, heavy eyes, not to behold
> This shameful lodging.
> Fortune, good night; smile once more; turn thy wheel! (ii. 170-3)

Edgar's soliloquy in scene iii is an obvious anticipation of Lear's
subsequent experience. He determines

> To take the basest and most poorest shape
> That ever penury, in contempt of man,
> Brought near to beast. (7-9)

But the difference between this and Lear is characteristic: Edgar, under
strong pressure, simulates this state. He *plans* to be a beggar as much as

Edmund plans to be an earl. Lear on the other hand is forced by circumstances and impulse to his nakedness, as Cordelia became a queen for love of her husband.

Deceived Affection: Lear (II. iv)

Hence the distinction between reason and affection becomes one of the distinctions between sub- and main plot. Its exploration is the special concern of Act II. How it relates to the play's general concerns is sufficiently obvious, and at the end of the Act it becomes directly engaged with them. Lear's hints of madness—'down, thou climbing sorrow'—grow towards the moment of Goneril's entrance, which provokes a recapitulation of the last scene between them, picking up as it were the threads of the first Act in another prayer to curse her—'O Heavens, If you do love old men . . .'. Lear still speaks for an order in nature which is more than Fortune's wheel, and tries to affirm it in rescinding his violence:

> I prithee, daughter, do not make me mad:
> I will not trouble thee, my child; farewell . . .
> Let shame come when it will, I do not call it;
> I do not bid the thunder-bearer shoot,
> Nor tell tales of thee to high-judging Jove. (iv. 220-30)

High-judging Jove takes no action; but the daughters do, in rapidly accelerating dispossession of all Lear's fallen state:

> What need you five-and-twenty, ten, or five,
> To follow in a house where twice so many
> Have a command to tend you?
> Reg.   What need one?
> Lear. O! reason not the need; our basest beggars
> Are in the poorest thing superfluous:
> Allow not nature more than nature needs,
> Man's life is cheap as beast's. Thou art a lady;
> If only to go warm were gorgeous,
> Why, nature needs not what thou gorgeous wear'st,
> Which scarcely keeps thee warm. But, for true need,—
> You Heavens, give me that patience, patience I need! (263-73)

The rhythmic drive through Goneril's and Regan's argument builds up the tension which explodes in Lear's first words, and carries on throughout his speech. In feeling that, we are obliged to feel also that such a rhythm is no part of the reasonableness the sisters' words protest: their reason has a passionate momentum, driven by a will to destructive cruelty. In this it is unlike Edmund's coolmindedness. The difference emerges later in their lust for him, which he can manipulate, but which leads them to destroy each other.

This tremendous rhythmic climax is simultaneously a dramatic climax, as Lear is reduced to a penury such as Edgar chose (the verbal echoes stress this point); and a thematic climax, in the definition of man's relation to nature. He is of it, but all that is distinctively his—*human* values—are 'superfluous' to nature. Man's life is cheap as beast's; his value is what he adds to it, a 'garment'. The idea of clothing here goes beyond decoration, or even warmth, to become an image of what makes man more than beast. But Lear is deprived of superfluity, nature itself is threatened: the beast's life has to be fathomed before the garment can be made. Mere 'need' is all the part of nature in man; morality is superfluous (as Regan's immorality—her décolleté dress—is also superfluous). The Nature Lear had stood for, the beneficent Goddess of Order, is lost here at last, cracks up in the first audible 'Storm and Tempest' that accompanies Lear's final conviction:

O Fool! I shall go mad. (288)

Act III: Storm

Interlude: Kent (III. i)

Act II has only a brief conclusion after its climax, hardly relaxing enough to let us enjoy an interval in the bar. Act III, however, opens with a choric scene which does effect a contrast in mood. Not a total contrast, because the storm is still audible; but against the sense of storm is set an epic-style verse which first contains the violence (sets it, as it were, at a distance) and proceeds to develop the suggestion of an ultimate resolution:

> But, true it is, from France there comes a power
> Into this scatter'd kingdom; who already,
> Wise in our negligence, have secret feet
> In some of our best ports, and are at point
> To show their open banner. Now to you:
> If on my credit you dare build so far
> To make your speed to Dover, you shall find
> Some that will thank you . . . (i. 30-37)

'Scatter'd kingdom' embraces simultaneously the political kingdom, the elements, and Lear's 'little world of man', scattered with his wits. Dover re-echoes through the next two Acts as an emblem of renewal, towards which everyone moves as towards the light at the end of a tunnel. It functions, effectively enough, as an arbitrary symbol derived simply from the facts of the story, and given significance by its context, and by the harmonious rhythms that go with it (though it may also carry associations of a 'port in a storm', together with its traditional place as 'home' to English travellers abroad). Thus a regenerative movement is set going (developing from Kent's soliloquy in II. ii) before the storm reaches its full violence. That violence will not, we are assured, be the play's final comment; an impulse towards tragi-comedy (implying a happy ending) is felt already here, and it will grow strongly in Act IV. But in Act V, it will be reversed, or largely so. To grasp that rejection, we have to grasp a sense of its fitness, to feel from its inception that the storm is too radical a disturbance of world and mind to reach so easy a resolution. Hence this initial glimpse of reconciliation becomes only partly consolatory: its placing before the full storm makes us aware of its fragility, how far beyond the probability of restoration the scattering goes.

The Cruelty of the Elements: Lear's Mind (III. ii-vi)

The storm itself is given in three parts, separated by brief tactical scenes—iii and v—concerning Edmund's affairs. The movement through Lear's three scenes is a progressive diminuendo of power (with a corresponding increase of pathos) commencing with the tremendous rant of scene ii:

> Blow, winds, and crack your cheeks! rage! blow! . . .
> Crack Nature's moulds, all germens spill at once
> That makes ingrateful man! (1-9)

and moving from that into the quieter (and more painful) verse of scene iv:

> Thou think'st 'tis much that this contentious storm
> Invades us to the skin: so 'tis to thee;
> But where the greater malady is fix'd,
> The lesser is scarce felt. Thou'ldst shun a bear;
> But if thy flight lay toward the roaring sea,
> Thou'ldst meet the bear i' th' mouth. When the mind's free
> The body's delicate; this tempest in my mind
> Doth from my senses take all feeling else
> Save what beats there—filial ingratitude! (6-14)

This in turn gives way to a verse that is scarcely more than prose, and finally to prose itself at the end of iv, and in scene vi.

This progressive lowering of the poetic pitch accompanies a double development in Lear's mind, so that we value it in opposite ways at once. The prose we end up with is at once calmer, and more mad. The growing calm of judgement sees more clearly; even in scene ii there are glimpses of this:

> Rumble thy bellyful! Spit, fire! spout, rain!
> Nor rain, wind, thunder, fire, are my daughters:
> I tax you not, you elements, with unkindness;
> I never gave you kingdom, call'd you children,
> You owe me no subscription: then let fall
> Your horrible pleasure; here I stand, your slave,
> A poor, infirm, weak, and despis'd old man. (14-20)

The pride seems to be turning towards self-pity, but there is also in that last line the quieter force of a statement of fact. For Lear, the assurance of interconnection between man and nature is breaking down: the sadism of the elements—their horrible pleasure—may image that of his daughters; but it is impersonal, not really related to them. The moral life of man (ingratitude) is dimly perceived here as something distinct from the processes of nature: the storm's violence is simply violence, not unkindness. In that sense, again, morality is recognised as a superfluity. This offers, in the growing quiet, a way of coming to terms with nature; but in that recognition the whole Elizabethan concept of a grand order,

C

in which the moral life of man is involved in a divinely ordained universe, is cracked and lost.

On the one hand, this offers a chance of quiet, for the offence shrinks from the universal to the private; but at the same time, justice itself is deprived of its general sanction. Lear is thrown back on human cruelty with no ultimate power to redeem it:

> No, I will weep no more. In such a night
> To shut me out? Pour on; I will endure.
> In such a night as this? O Regan, Goneril!
> Your old kind father, whose frank heart gave all,—
> O! that way madness lies; let me shun that;
> No more of that. (iv. 17-22)

What is in one sense a chance of calm, is in another a stronger drive to madness. Lear is still struggling to link his new perception of humanity with a tenable concept of justice:

> Poor naked wretches, whereso'er you are,
> That bide the pelting of this pitiless storm,
> How shall your houseless heads and unfed sides,
> Your loop'd and window'd raggedness, defend you
> From seasons such as these? O! I have ta'en
> Too little care of this. Take physic, Pomp;
> Expose thyself to feel what wretches feel,
> That thou mayst shake the superflux to them,
> And show the Heavens more just. (28-36)

The beggars' clothing here, picking up the image from 'O! reason not the need', is simply for protection, a shelter like a house. Lear turns from the general vision of man's vulnerability, to a political justice in the distribution of wealth; offering his experience emblemised as a mirror for magistrates, to shake the superflux to poverty. But the expedient is desperate that leads from the moment of clarity, 'I have ta'en Too little care of this' into a claim to 'show the Heavens more just' by shaking the superflux. Desperate, because there is here no superflux to shake, 'loop'd and window'd raggedness' is Lear himself as well as the beggar.

So it is at this moment that Poor Tom is brought into the scene, the physical presence of what Lear has just imagined. A loop'd and window'd raggedness of mind as well as body (the complexity of the scene is increased by our knowledge that Tom is only an image, not a fact; Edgar is simulating his madness). This sight drives Lear to the last perception, the bare prosaic fact:

> Is man no more than this? Consider him well. Thou ow'st the worm no silk, the beast no hide, the sheep no wool, the cat no perfume. Ha! here's three on's are sophisticated; thou are the thing itself; unaccommodated man is no more but such a poor, bare, forked animal as thou art. Off, off, you lendings! Come; unbutton here. (105-12)

Lear does not shake the superflux to Tom; he sees a reflection of himself, accommodated only by lendings that have lost their value. Man, detached from his place in the grand order, has no superflux to shake. Expecting no more, we can contemplate his unaccommodated condition; but we cannot value it.

Hence the clarity of vision to which Lear has been approaching comes to seeing nothing at all, like the Fool. This is at once the rock bottom from which reconstruction can begin, and the utter deprivation in which sanity has no meaning. Lear is brought to the natural state of the Fool (who disappears after this Act), and Merlin's prophecy with which the Fool ended scene ii, of a handy-dandy world where all evil becomes good, is fulfilled in the mock trial where justice is a ludicrous pretence, a dressing-up:

> Thou robed man of justice, take thy place. (vi. 37)

The grand order of nature has been destroyed, and all discord follows. Political society is chaos, the little world of man has no stability, and the distinction of sanity and insanity disappears as Lear sets a lunatic and a Fool to judge his daughters.

I noted that the descent from the roaring verse of scene ii to this cracked prose involved a double movement: towards calm, and towards a state in which no settled calm is possible. Both are contained in Kent's valediction:

> Oppressed nature sleeps.
> This rest might yet have balm'd thy broken sinews
> Which, if convenience will not allow,
> Stand in hard cure. (100-3)

Such a sleep is either peace, or exhaustion; or, in fact, both.

The Cruelty of Man: Gloucester's Eyes (III. vii)

The end of Act III is the equivalent devastation of Gloucester: the physical horror of watching his eyes put out. Edgar has assured us that mental torture is worse than physical: 'Who alone suffers, suffers most i' th' mind' (vi. 107). In confident couplets, this truth is shrouded in complacency. It *is* true; but it cannot be known smugly. Seeing Gloucester's eyes out is more immediately horrible than anything so far; hence it rams home all that we have had: the capacity of man for beastliness, and the greaterness of Lear's suffering than this so obvious horror. It is needed in the play, to make us see. Yet, at the same time, for all its vileness, Gloucester's fate does not challenge the order of things: we know what's right, what's wrong here, as we do not with Lear; and that, too, marks the difference of depth. The regenerative impulse can proceed straightforwardly for Gloucester, as it cannot for Lear. Gloucester will 'see more clearly' when blind; what Lear sees more clearly makes him blinder still: a poor, bare, forked animal, no more at all.

Act IV: Sunshine and Rain at once

The movement towards reconstruction, or regeneration, which I noted as present in Act III, reaches successive culminations in Act IV, first for Gloucester, then for Lear. For both of them it is preceded by exhaustion of mind following their experiences in Act III, and so by declarations of despair. Such a process can be interpreted in a variety of ways, ranging from the fatalistic idea of the turning of Fortune's wheel (suggested by Kent's words earlier) to the Christian idea of redemption. For both these, warrant can be found in the text, in allusions and hints; but stronger than either is the sense of nature, internal and external, as immediate experience on which any superstructure of interpretation may be mere delusion. The dominant image is still of the storm, or rather the aftermath of storm, the renewed freshness of the world, watery but astonishingly hopeful; and as Lear's latest madness is to appear dressed as a May-king, the image of nature extends towards the emergence of spring from winter. These ideas are cyclical, but they are not the arbitrary turning of Fortune's wheel; and they may even seem 'miraculous' as the cessation of despair, or the passing of a storm, is always unexpected. But the resources of these miracles are not supernatural; the power of this Act rests with the extraordinarily convincing psychological movement echoing that of the natural world.

Good Reason: Edgar and Gloucester (IV. i)

The rôle of master of the ceremonies rested with Edmund in the destructive movement of Act II; it passes here to Edgar, announcing a turn for the better:

> The lamentable change is from the best;
> The worst returns to laughter. (i. 5-6)

There is about this a curiously smug tone, to which Edgar returns at intervals. He offers a simple moralising of disaster, not far removed from the disarming assurance of Pope's 'whatever is, is right'. He is immediately shocked into less confident thoughts by the sight of his father; but the moralising tone is in Gloucester's utterance as well:

> I have no way, and therefore want no eyes;
> I stumbled when I saw. Full oft 'tis seen,
> Our means secure us, and our mere defects
> Prove our commodities. Oh! dear son Edgar,
> The food of thy abused father's wrath;
> Might I but live to see thee in my touch,
> I'd say I had eyes again. (18-24)

This, one feels, is the poetry of tragi-comedy; at such a level of thought and experience nothing goes deep enough for tragedy. This quality is emphasised by the element of fanciful absurdity in the stage situation: Edgar is there, and could be touched, if he would reveal himself. That he does not, can only prolong Gloucester's pain; yet Shakespeare's efforts to make this plausible seem curiously perfunctory. In IV. vi Edgar tells us:

> Why I do trifle thus with his despair
> Is done to cure it. (33-34)

and in V. iii, when Gloucester is dead and therefore no longer present
to make us feel the inadequacy of the apology, we are told that
Edgar:

> Led him, begg'd for him, sav'd him from despair;
> Never—O fault!—reveal'd myself unto him,
> Until some half-hour past . . . (191-3)

We are not always so conscious of this while watching the play, because
the pain which Edgar registers in his frequent asides preserves him in our
sympathies. But it is dramatically the most questionable thing in the
play; and it is also the point at which that disregard for normal probability which I compared in my prologue to Shakespeare's last plays is
most conspicuous. Edgar and Gloucester in Act IV enact a simple moral
exemplum; the function of their presence on the stage is essentially like
the tone of their speeches; and it may be through this perception that we
can best understand their improbability. By contrast with them, all that
we see of Lear is infinitely more natural, and less moral. Edgar and
Gloucester give us what the play would be, if it were a moralising tragi-
comedy (when Shakespeare does write such a play, *The Winter's Tale*, he
does it far more persuasively); the contrast between sub-plot and main
plot here is one of genre as well as depth.

Hence, within this dominant complacency of tone, this obviously
soluble despair, Gloucester's famous lines—

> As flies to wanton boys, are we to th' Gods;
> They kill us for their sport. (IV. i. 36-37)

—have not in their context quite the same force they have out of it. As
Gloucester speaks, his words are contained within our understanding
that they will be answered.

Answered, that is, for Gloucester. But here, interconnection between
the two plots becomes vital. In the thematic equivalence between them,
cross-reference is inevitable; and the aphoristic tendency in Gloucester's
speech as well as Edgar's tends to leave their words remembered out of

context, to remain with us as we watch Lear. Hence Gloucester's words of despair may not cut deep applied to himself, but are far more serious as they reflect on Lear. It is, in fact, men who have sported with Gloucester, the gods have attended to Lear; that Gloucester's despair can be relieved only makes it plainer that Lear's cannot. So that all the argument here has a double value, almost a kind of irony: it means one thing about Gloucester, but another about Lear. And Edgar's moral tone, offered as comfort to the one, seems, in relation to the other, harsh and false.

Such a reflection on the rôle he plays with his father is in fact suggested by Edgar himself, in his asides:

> O Gods! Who is't can say 'I am at the worst'?
> I am worse than e'er I was.
> Old Man.   'Tis poor mad Tom.
> Edg. [Aside.] And worse I may be yet; the worst is not
>   So long as we can say 'This is the worst.' (i. 25-28)

In that reflection we understand the element of play-acting in Edgar's relations with his father; and we are warned that the play itself will not be tragi-comedy. Yet we know now, or are soon shown, that Gloucester does come to a recognisable 'worst', and so rises from it. At the same time we are forced to see that whatever Gloucester is, Lear is 'worse'. When that is understood, the fatalistic notion of the wheel of Fortune seems actually optimistic; it suggests an inevitable return from the worst, and that may be false to experience. On this conception rests the contrast of Acts IV and V: in IV it is continually suggested that the wheel is turning up at last, that the worst has been. But in V worse still is given.

The complacent movement, in verse and action, apparent in Act IV, has disturbing undercurrents; it is not likely to prove conclusive. It is, however, very powerful. I said that Edgar takes over from Edmund the rôle of master of ceremonies, not as Machiavellian manipulator, but as a self-appointed agent of Providence. As that, he resumes his disguise as poor Tom to guide Gloucester towards 'sight'. Gloucester descants on his experience as Lear had done in the storm, but to significantly different effect:

>   That I am wretched
> Makes thee the happier: Heavens, deal so still!
> Let the superfluous and lust-dieted man,

That slaves your ordinance, that will not see
Because he does not feel, feel your power quickly;
So distribution should undo excess,
And each man have enough. Dost thou know Dover? (65–71)

Gloucester, like Lear, is attracted (as Danby remarked) to Protestant
ideas of communism current in the sixteenth century. But his facile
distinction of 'superfluous' from 'enough' reminds us of Lear's discovery
that all 'enough' is superfluity, so that *his* reaction to poor Tom was to
strip off his own clothes. Lear's action may have been mad, but it was
also clearer-sighted. We cannot, then, in that insistent echoing of Lear's
earlier speeches, mistake this notion of a simply efficient Providence for
a system of belief adequate to the full experience of the play. The diffi-
culty of commenting is that while we are not to find it adequate, we are
nevertheless obliged to take it seriously.

Evil Passion: Goneril (IV. ii)

One kind of counterbalance to the possible cosiness of Gloucester's
scenes is the increasingly disturbing force of passion revealed in Goneril
and Regan, and their lust for Edmund. Goneril's 'lust-diet' is not a
superfluity which can be distributed; it is a homogeneous force of appalling evil, and so provokes Albany's concentration of animal imagery
which culminates in:

> If that the heavens do not their visible spirits
> Send quickly down to tame these vilde offences,
> It will come,
> Humanity must perforce prey on itself,
> Like monsters of the deep. (ii. 46–50)

Man's part in nature here is vilde, beyond human control (even Edgar's);
it can be solved only by divine intervention, which is not forthcoming.
But just as Edgar seeks consolation in the idea of beneficent gods, so
Albany will cheer himself up with belief in vengeful heavens:

Mess.   O! my good Lord, the Duke of Cornwall's dead;
           Slain by his servant, going to put out
           The other eye of Gloucester. (70–72)

Alb.   This shows you are above,
              You justicers, that these our nether crimes
              So speedily can venge! (78-80)

The smooth sweep to that generalisation betrays the urgent need to
believe, even in punitive deities. Given all that we have seen in the play,
we are bound to resist this. Cornwall's death may be taken as divine
retribution; it can equally be seen as humanity preying on itself. What
we took it for at the time was a positive assertion of values defended by
the servant: a glimpse, not of justice, but of human decency.

Interlude: Kent and Cordelia (IV. iii and iv)

   The same feeling is enlarged upon in the choric scene (iii) between
Kent and the Gentleman, discussing Cordelia's landing and behaviour.
Here, on a much larger scale, is the impulse that moved the servant to
kill Cornwall. The Gentleman links it with the process of nature in the
play:

Kent.   O! then it mov'd her.
Gent.   Not to a rage; patience and sorrow strove
           Who should express her goodliest. You have seen
           Sunshine and rain at once. (16-19)

Sunshine and rain at once is a sequel to the storm; or if one takes it as a
spring shower it is the sequel to the devastations of winter. Either way,
the feeling is strongly conveyed of their co-existence in nature, giving us
a (much-needed) confidence that Cordelia is as probable as Goneril, not
an extraordinary special case. A similar imagery is sustained in the next
scene, when Cordelia describes Lear 'mad as the vex'd sea', crowned
with 'all the idle weeds that grow In our sustaining corn'. The Doctor
sums up this mood with 'Our foster-nurse of nature is repose', and in
this stress on the pleasant weeds is felt again the idea of superfluity as a
principle of nature. Not an issue of Justice, or Providence, or Fate, or
any grand Order, but simply an equal and opposite fact to the beasts of
prey. This, in fact, is the answer to Kent's words just before:

                    It is the stars,
              The stars above us, govern our conditions;
              Else one self mate and make could not beget
              Such different issues. (iii. 33-36)

This could refer to Lear, or to nature, or to both. In any case, the proposition is made in a way which invites contradiction: the fact to be faced is that Lear and nature *do* beget such different issues. But the whole movement at this point is from the vilde towards the good in nature, on which depends the regenerative force of the Act. Such a movement as we are shown does not endorse the influence of the stars, any more than confidence in Justice; it only reveals what such illusions may derive from. Why do men think the Universe is just? Because it is sometimes kind.

Regeneration: Gloucester (IV. vi. 1-80)

The first part of Act IV develops this movement towards regeneration, with continual ironic cross-reference between the two plots, and more direct reminders of unregenerate nature. The second part—scenes vi and vii—presents the regenerative experiences themselves. They are very different in style, idea and tone, and again their juxtaposition compels critical cross-reference.

Gloucester and Edgar approach—supposedly—Dover cliff, in a verse of heightened confidence, as Gloucester notices:

> Methinks thy voice is alter'd, and thou speak'st
> In better phrase and matter than thou didst. (vi. 7-8)

Edgar uses his 'better phrase and matter' for a god's-eye view of mice-like men:

> Come on, sir; here's the place: stand still. How fearful
> And dizzy 'tis to cast one's eyes so low!
> The crows and choughs that wing the midway air
> Show scarce so gross as beetles; half way down
> Hangs one that gathers sampire, dreadful trade!
> Methinks he seems no bigger than his head.
> The fishermen that walk upon the beach
> Appear like mice, and yond tall anchoring bark
> Diminish'd to her cock, her cock a buoy
> Almost too small for sight. The murmuring surge,
> That on th' unnumber'd idle pebble chafes,
> Cannot be heard so high. (11-22)

The leisured, expansive rhythm and detailed imagery all enforce the sense of this as an ordered world, whose petty strifes are ridiculous if not invisible to the distant viewer. Its peculiar effect in the theatre (less obvious when read) is that what Edgar describes so vividly is not really happening at all. This is part of the elaborate play-acting between him and Gloucester which culminates in the mock-suicide twenty lines later. Edgar has assumed the divine rôle to prove his point:

> Think that the clearest Gods, who make them honours
> Of men's impossibilities, have preserved thee. (73-74)

'Clearest Gods' is a distinct affirmation, within the limiting context of this make-believe, of their existence, their justice, and so of the orthodox natural order. But it depends, not on natural experience, but on the moral allegory that Edgar has contrived. Gloucester acknowledges the lesson:

> I do remember now; henceforth I'll bear
> Affliction till it do cry out itself
> 'Enough, enough,' and die. (75-77)

The point (to be echoed later in Edgar's 'Ripeness is all') is impressively made; but here again reference to Lear becomes inevitable. Lear's affliction has driven him mad; that is, beyond the choice of dying or not dying, and beyond the reach of Edgar's didactic tone: 'Bear free and patient thoughts.' (80)

Desperation: Lear (IV. vi. 81-288)

In other words, this climax of Gloucester's education is the cue for Lear's entry, which he makes—more completely mad than ever before —'fantastically dressed with wild flowers'. The 'side-piercing sight' questions the measured affirmation which has just been given, and our questioning grows in urgency as Lear's madness comes to some coherence in violent detestation of all natural life, specifically sexual life:

> To't, Luxury, pell-mell!
> For I lack soldiers. Behold yond simp'ring dame,
> Whose face between her forks presages snow;
> That minces virtue, and does shake the head
> To hear of pleasure's name;

> The fitchew nor the soiled horse goes to't
> With a more riotous appetite.
> Down from the waist they are Centaurs,
> Though women all above. (119-27)

The words are general; but we have seen Goneril just this. Lear's sex-disgust is to be recognised as a condition of his madness; but he is generalising from genuine particulars. What for did Edgar's clearest gods make Goneril?

Lear's life-hatred grows in explicitness.

Glou.   O! let me kiss that hand.
Lear.   Let me wipe it first; it smells of mortality. (134-5)

This proceeds through prose on the theme 'handy-dandy, which is the justice, which is the thief?' to a growing rhythmic emphasis in verse:

> There thou might'st behold
> The great image of Authority:
> A dog's obey'd in office. (159-61)

Edgar comments 'matter and impertinency mix'd; Reason in madness'. He is right, but, handy-dandy, one reflects how much madness and impertinency there was in Edgar's reason. Lear ends the scene with his power of words reduced (as often in the last two Acts) to the bare articulation of a key-word:

> Then, kill, kill, kill, kill, kill, kill! (189)

It is not surprising, after this, to find Gloucester wanting to die again; nor can one miss the irony that a brief while later it is *Edgar* who does the first killing (of Oswald), commenting on his embarrassment:

> He's dead; I am only sorry
> He had no other deathsman. (259-60)

Edgar has lost our confidence as moral demonstrator, and the rest of the Act is in other hands, indicated by the Gentleman:

> Thou hast one daughter,
> Who redeems nature from the general curse
> Which twain have brought her to. (206-8)

Goneril and Regan have brought Lear to curse nature generally; Cordelia must redeem his sense of good. And, if one takes 'twain' to hint at Adam and Eve,[1] her doing so will resemble the Christian redemption of the general curse on nature.

Regeneration: Lear (IV. vii)

What we feel as the inadequacy of Gloucester's reform in the presence of Lear is, at least in part, a contrast between morality and nature. Gloucester confronts a moral state of man with the assumption that all partial evil is universal good. Lear's condition, his involvement with natural forces, represents a superfluity of evil; a context in which the moral choices of men tend to lose significance. Hence a radically different sense of regeneration is developed, one whose bearings are so much more natural than moral that it rather contradicts than supplements Edgar's sententiae.

This is achieved by the sharp change in verse-mode which I noted in my prologue:

> Cor.   O you kind Gods,
> Cure this great breach in his abused nature!
> Th' untuned and jarring senses, O! wind up
> Of this child-changed father. (vii. 14-17)

It is precisely this musical image which governs what follows, indicating not a moral choice, but the direct experience of contrast between tune-lessness and tune, chaos and harmony, cruelty and tenderness—rooted in the sense of nature, both by 'abused nature' and by 'child-changed'. Whether that means 'changed by children' or 'changed into a child', or both, it lays the stress on the closest *natural* relationship.

Cordelia recalls the storm world of Act III, the jarring sense that is to be tuned as Lear wakes up; his first words jar still:

---

[1] Muir comments: 'Not Adam and Eve, as Danby fancifully suggests, but Goneril and Regan.' The lines seem naturally to imply both.

> You do me wrong to take me out o' th' grave;
> Thou art a soul in bliss; but I am bound
> Upon a wheel of fire, that mine own tears
> Do scald like molten lead. (45-48)

He speaks of heaven and hell, and the source of his agony is con-
science; but the terms are rather of bliss and torture than of good and
evil.

The musical re-formation is achieved as the verse changes, to Lear'
supremely memorable recognition of Cordelia:

> Do not laugh at me;
> For, as I am a man, I think this lady
> To be my child Cordelia.

Cor.   And so I am, I am. (68-70)

The tone of the utterance conveys the sense of harmony, as surely as it
words redeem 'child-changed' to the tremendous affirmation of 'And
so I am, I am.'

It has frequently been pointed out that here Lear achieves the self
knowledge he earlier lacked; that this is sight after blindness, when h
recognises Cordelia. This is true; but a simple moral stress is out of place
Lear's penitence is as excessive as his violence; action and reaction ar
equal and opposite. Moral contrition is a condition of this re-vision, bu
it does not 'explain' it:

> Be your tears wet? Yes, faith. I pray, weep not:
> If you have poison for me, I will drink it.
> I know you do not love me; for your sisters
> Have, as I do remember, done me wrong:
> You have some cause, they have not.

Cor.   No cause, no cause. (71-75)

The significance of this, I suggest, is precisely that it is not clear-sighted
Cordelia *had* cause. Her love exceeds the facts as utterly as Lear's hatre
did. She, too, has changed: the half and half division of love that sh
proposed for her bond in Act I was meaningless; she can love both fathe
and husband, but not by fractions. What Lear is being brought to see
not the unbearable facts, but a superfluity of good in nature which ca

transcend the facts. This is not an argument for a grand order or an ultimate salvation, but a revelation of forces opposite to the monsters of the deep. The good that exists is a matter, not of justice, but of superfluity. Lear's recognition of Cordelia takes symbolic effect from its human power as a recognition, not of his fault, but of the living power of affection. His acknowledgement of it is slow, and painful: 'Do not abuse me.' But when we see him next, his confidence in Cordelia is perfect.

The tremendous power of this affirmation may easily blind us to its frailty; but that too is felt in the verse in which it is made. The grasping of the reality of this impulse to harmony as a force in nature opposite to destructive violence does not make the latter unreal; nor does it make the forces equal.

Act V: Dead as Earth

After Lear and Cordelia have left the stage, a few lines of prose remind us that their future rests, not only on the delicate balance of their personal relationship, but also on the less predictable fortunes of the battle Cordelia has come to fight:

Kent.   My point and period will be throughly wrought,
        Or well or ill, as this day's battle's fought. (IV. vii. 95-96)

The rather perfunctory couplet is not likely to disturb our relief much. Rather, it emphasises the seeming unimportance of what would more conventionally (for instance in Shakespeare's earlier history plays) be the major action. Yet the battle does represent the larger frame of action, and in it Edgar and Albany expect to see the frame of nature endorsed by the just action of the gods. The idea may seem trivial and crude; but it should be recognised that it is the play's concentration on profound personal experience which conditions our impatience here. As the play is read, one may almost overlook the battle altogether, for it is achieved in two stage directions during the eleven lines of scene ii; over so fast and with so little emphasis that it resembles the strangely unobtrusive crises of murder or rape in E. M. Forster's novels. On the stage it is not so inconspicuous, for the directions call for full processions to march across the stage in attack and retreat: in other words, an impressive dumb show of hope and failure takes place. But it is still strange, in that no fighting seems to be called for on the stage, and the acting-time that can reasonably be given to it is very short indeed. Thus, it seems rather to symbolise its own irrelevance than to dramatise a larger issue. By itself, this will have no power to disturb the reassurance of the end of Act IV.

Lust: Goneril and Regan (V. i)

But the opening of Act V does redress the balance, in another way: by revealing the conflict of lust between Goneril and Regan it exposes a force that is as 'natural' and as powerful as the love of Lear and Cordelia; and as much as that was creative and encouraging, this is destructive and appalling. But one self mate and make did beget such different issues; they are equally rooted in nature, and in Lear. The development of Goneril and Regan that I noted earlier is completed here; their hypocrisy, and seeming reasonableness, were revealed as passion-driven in Act II, and Regan derived a horrid pleasure from putting Gloucester's eyes out that exceeded her husband's crude brutality. Now the contrast between them and Edmund is finally clear: his cool reason remains unaffected by the naked lust which makes them, monsters of the deep, prey upon each other. Their evil does indeed work itself out: in scene iii Regan is poisoned, Goneril discredited and dead. Their fawning over Edmund and snarling at each other emerge only in fragmentary speech, reflected in the anger and contempt of Albany. On the stage they are often represented as less comic versions of Cinderella's ugly sisters; this is not inappropriate, but the sensuality must be dominant. The nastiest evil in its nature destroys itself, but it does not therefore cease to inhere in nature; and it destroys other things too. The legacy of Goneril and Regan is to emerge, via Edmund's slow surrender, in Cordelia's death. Their bodies are brought on, and the dying Edmund is touched by ironic understanding: 'Yet Edmund was belov'd' (iii. 239). His reaction is, of course, too late: fifteen lines later, Lear enters with Cordelia dead in his arms. No good comes of this evil.

Act V, altogether, is constructed on a see-saw between right and wrong, as moral qualities of man, and between good and evil as forces inherent in nature. At any given moment it may seem to come to a limited conclusion. 'Good' dominates with Cordelia, or 'right' with

Albany; 'wrong' with Edmund, 'evil' with Goneril; and these successive dominations ironically balance each other until the final composition achieves a definition which alone satisfies the complex understanding of the whole play. But by then we shall find it hard to use the terms 'good' and 'evil', still less 'right' and 'wrong', with any assurance of their value.

Ripeness is All: Edgar and Gloucester (V. ii)

The first movement blasts the regenerative sense in which Act IV concluded. And 'Dover', which has stood since Act II as the emblem of hope and the restoration of order, is briefly but finally disposed of in the symbolic battle of scene ii. Cordelia's army is defeated; but in this disappointment, bitter to Gloucester, Edgar finds his essential moral:

Glou.	No further, sir; a man may rot even here.
Edg.	What! in ill thoughts again? Men must endure
	Their going hence, even as their coming hither:
	Ripeness is all. Come on.
Glou.	And that's true too. (ii. 8-11)

'Ripeness' here has been subject to various interpretations. At its simplest, it means 'readiness', that men must be prepared to die. But its remarkable evocative power, what causes such frequent comment on it, clearly involves more than that; in contrast to Gloucester's word 'rot' it suggests the perfect maturity of fruit, a point of achievement at which death may be more appropriate than decay. Muir quotes a very pertinent passage from Elyot's *The Gouernour*:

in such astate that it may neyther encrease nor minysshe without losinge the denomination of Maturitie . . . ripe or redy, as fruite when it is ripe, it is at the very poynte to be gathered and eaten.

It is not surprising that in a play so persistently concerned both with old age and with nature, this phrase has such powerful reverberations. It has the ring of a conclusive cadence: this might be the final judgement of a stoic tragedy, marking the point at which regret for the hero's death gives place to satisfaction at his achievement. It is, in fact, frequently lifted out of its context and offered as a judgement on this play's ending. But it can seem to be that, only because of its singular power; Edgar achieves a conjuring trick with words, not unlike Milton's at the end of

Samson Agonistes, when Samson speaks of 'Calm of mind, all passion spent' in the same breath as rejoicing at the destruction of his enemies. The validity of Edgar's cadence depends on the 'ripeness' that we actually feel in Gloucester, as in Lear.

Birds i' th' Cage: Lear and Cordelia (V. iii. 1-40)

Hence, as in the analogous moment in IV. vi, it is the cue for Lear's entry:

> Shall we not see these daughters and these sisters?
> *Lear.* No, no, no, no! Come, let's away to prison;
> We two alone will sing like birds i' th' cage. (iii. 7-9)

Lear's refusal to see evil, and the image he offers, as well as the lightness of rhythm in which it is expressed, offer an emblem of something desperately unlike ripeness. The gaiety of the caged bird is born of irresponsibility, of lost contact with its natural environment. For a moment it becomes an enchanting vision, repeating endlessly the mood of IV. vii:

> When thou dost ask me blessing, I'll kneel down,
> And ask of thee forgiveness: (10-11)

But this transposes into the futility of such a prospect:

> so we'll live,
> And pray, and sing, and tell old tales, and laugh
> At gilded butterflies, and hear poor rogues
> Talk of court news; and we'll talk with them too,
> Who loses and who wins; who's in, who's out;
> And take upon's the mystery of things,
> As if we were God's spies: (11-17)

In the context of this brittle gaiety, the 'mystery of things' refers primarily to court politics, and only ironically to the larger mystery represented by 'God's spies'. In that last word, the bitter undertone of all this comes out, and the remainder of the speech dwells on the cage in which the birds are constrained to sing:

> and we'll wear out,
> In a wall'd prison, packs and sects of great ones
> That ebb and flow by th' moon. (17-19)

Lear's idyll is not the sustaining of the mood of IV. vii, but the painful recognition of its collapse; its undertone comes through in the vindictive violence of his next speech (partly made up of phrases from the Old Testament):

> Upon such sacrifices, my Cordelia,
> The Gods themselves throw incense. Have I caught thee?
> He that parts us shall bring a brand from heaven,
> And fire us hence like foxes. Wipe thine eyes;
> The good years shall devour them, flesh and fell,
> Ere they shall make us weep: we'll see 'em starv'd first. (20-25)

This is, of course, a very moving declaration of the repose Lear finds in Cordelia; but that sense barely contains his anger. His passion is very far from spent.

They leave the stage, and Edmund prepares their murder. Lear has revived the animal imagery, and the officer's response to Edmund's order is a perfect ironic comment on the relations of men and beasts:

> I cannot draw a cart nor eat dried oats;
> If it be man's work I'll do't. (39-40)

It is man's work; and he does it.

The Gods are Just: Edgar and Edmund (V. iii. 41-221)

But in the meantime, Edgar has another conclusion to press. In scene ii he offered a stoic coda for the play, but scene iii proceeded past that; now he appears in a heroic rôle. One can see the process of this Act as a succession of codas of different kinds, each made familiar by other Elizabethan tragedies; and each invalidated by what follows. Edgar's appearance in shining armour recalls scenes of jousting in the history plays, and the verse has a similarly reminiscent splendour. The lost battle, which called for stoic endurance, is reversed in victorious personal combat; and the implication of this success is a new confidence in the beneficent order of things:

> Let's exchange charity.
> I am no less in blood than thou art, Edmund;
> If more, the more th' hast wrong'd me.
> My name is Edgar, and thy father's son.
> The Gods are just, and of our pleasant vices
> Make instruments to plague us;
> The dark and vicious place where thee he got
> Cost him his eyes. (166–73)

The 'charity' which understands 'justice' in such vindictive terms cannot command our assent. This is Edgar's final affirmation of the Gods, finding evidence of their existence in the moral justification of events. Such a thing can be said of Gloucester: his story has always been an exemplum of poetic justice; but it is very offensive, even about him. It could not be said at all of Lear. But even for Gloucester, the moralistic pattern is incomplete. Edgar goes on to describe his death:

> his flaw'd heart,
> Alack, too weak the conflict to support!
> 'Twixt two extremes of passion, joy and grief,
> Burst smilingly. (196–9)

This death from the conflict of extremes of passion is the very reverse of the mature balance of passions that Elyot spoke of, envisaged in 'Ripeness is all'. And it is something in which the gods, just or otherwise, have no part. We are prepared now, not only to recognise that the grand order for which Edgar seeks has no validity; but also, that if it did exist, we should want no part of it. A moral concept of this kind becomes an affront to the human experience the play presents. The problem of the co-existence of good and evil cannot, as we see it here, be solved in moral terms of right and wrong; for the moment we may prefer Edmund's characteristically dispassionate conclusion: 'The wheel is come full circle; I am here.'

Heaven's Vault Cracks: Cordelia and Lear (V. iii. 222–326)

There the formal orthodox drama supporting the notion of poetic justice virtually ends: in ironic recognition of its inadequacy to the general sense of nature, or to the particular sense of the people. After this a happy ending could only be trivial, and therefore painful. The eighteenth-century versions of the play finished allegorically, by marry-

ing Edgar's severe justice to Cordelia's sweet charity; and if their belief
in natural order was to be sustained, this was the obvious way to do it.
Edgar's play, as we have seen, is allegorical in character; but we have
also seen that by contrast with it Lear's play seems always more natural,
and therefore more profound. The eighteenth-century solution was
sentimental, in turning away from the implications of experience.

Given the pattern of the play hitherto, we must expect a reversal of
Edgar's complacence. But the dramatic climax which Shakespeare
produces is far more powerful than we could expect. Albany repeats
Edgar's sentiments in more acceptable form, commenting on Goneril
and Regan's deaths:

> This judgment of the heavens, that makes us tremble,
> Touches us not with pity. (231-2)

Edmund confesses his plot to kill Cordelia, and Albany begs the Gods
defend her; then:

> *Re-enter* Lear, *with* Cordelia *dead in his arms.*
>
> Lear.   Howl, howl, howl! O! you are men of stones:
> Had I your tongues and eyes, I'd use them so
> That heaven's vault should crack. (257-9)

Which utterly blasts the last movement toward complacence. But
beyond that, the promise of regeneration is blasted too:

> She's gone for ever.
> I know when one is dead, and when one lives;
> She's dead as earth. (259-61)

This is the final point of Lear's clear sight. She and earth are dead; there
can be no regeneration from dead earth. The moral sequence that began
in Act I with Kent's 'See better, Lear' is concluded here: Lear's perfect
sight is rewarded with this.

That is the worst the play offers, and the process thereafter is away
from it, though not far away. Lear retreats into a sympathetic delusion,
because this barren truth is unbearable:

> This feather stirs; she lives! if it be so,
> It is a chance which does redeem all sorrows
> That ever I have felt. (265-7)

It is not so; and nothing is redeemed. It is, in fact, very much the un-redeemed Lear who scornfully rejects Kent and Edgar:

> A plague upon you, murderers, traitors all!
> I might have sav'd her; now she's gone for ever! (269-70)

His anger revives his energy, and for a moment the old Lear is heard again:

> I kill'd the slave that was a-hanging thee.
> *Offi.*   'Tis true, my lords, he did.
> *Lear.*   Did I not, fellow?
> I have seen the day, with my good biting falchion
> I would have made them skip. (274-7)

The boast has the energetic pride of Act I; the redemptive humility of IV. vii is displaced, but it would take a very determined moralist to regret the fact. When Lear does come to recognise Kent, it is in a return of exhaustion:

> I am old now,
> And these same crosses spoil me. Who are you?
> Mine eyes are not o' th' best: I'll tell you straight. (277-9)

Albany still tries to give the play a noble ending, resigning his power to 'this old Majesty', restoring Kent and Edgar to their earldoms, and promising justice to the realm:

> All friends shall taste
> The wages of their virtue, and all foes
> The cup of their deservings. (302-4)

That is the last of the play's false endings, the conventional gesture common to most tragedies of the time: *Hamlet*, *Othello*, *Macbeth*, all conclude with such a promise of restored order, however muted. But Albany continues:

> O! see, see!
> *Lear.*   And my poor fool is hang'd! No, no, no life! (304-5)

Lear means Cordelia, not the Fool; but the word is suggestive, not only

of the Fool's honesty, but also of the frailty which finally links Cordelia
to the Fool. The end is another bare repetition of a key-word:

> Thou'lt come no more,
> Never, never, never, never, never! (307-8)

From that knowledge, Lear retreats to:

> Do you see this? Look on her, look, her lips,
> Look there, look there!   *Dies.* (310-11)

The obvious meaning of this is the happiness of delusion, that Lear
dies believing Cordelia to be alive. 'The worst returns to laughter'; but
not as Edgar meant it. Other interpretations have been offered: that he
thinks he sees her soul issuing from her lips to heaven, in the way of
many renaissance paintings. But that would be, in this play, no less
illusory; there is no suggested consolation in a life after death. Only the
forcing us to see, with Lear, the unbearable truth of 'she's dead as earth';
after that, the rights and wrongs of compassion for his delusion are
irrelevant to the sense of need for it.[1]

Edgar's 'justice' became offensive; his moral optimism was a delusion.
Cordelia dies; and after that we can only be satisfied by facing the truth
of the ending. The play's last powerful visual impression is of Lear dying
with Cordelia dead in his arms. That justifies the last speech of the play,
the actual end when Edgar (or it may be Albany) offers no further
consolation:

> The weight of this sad time we must obey;
> Speak what we feel, not what we ought to say.
> The oldest hath borne most: we that are young
> Shall never see so much, nor live so long. (323-6)

What we *feel* is finally justified against all the moral impulses of what
we 'ought' to say. That applies to Lear's deluded death about which
what we ought to say ('See better, Lear'?) is unspeakable. The implications are, of course, profoundly moral; but not in any possible sense
reducible to conceptual terms.

---

[1] The last lines have also been held to mean that Lear does die knowing
the truth; that seems to be mere wishful thinking.

Epilogue

At the end of any play the lights go up and we shuffle out of the theatre. The normal world slowly reasserts itself. After a successful comedy, the gaiety may remain with us for some time; the horror of tragedy is usually shorter-lived: a brief quietness is followed by a resurgence of feeling. It does not require a subtle psychology to understand this; such a reaction is obviously to be expected. Most tragedies, in fact, supply a kind of warmth to set this reaction going: Oedipus, broken and blinded, is yet able to leave the stage on his own strength; Hamlet is dead, but we are to see him borne 'like a soldier, to the stage; For he was likely, had he been put on, To have prov'd most royally'. We may wonder uneasily how true that is; but it is not completely untrue, and it points the way our feelings want to go. This reaction, of course, is not confined to the theatre; after a funeral we are inclined to unseemly mirth. But then the reaction is complicated by guilt, the sense of disrespect for the dead; at the theatre there is no such guilt, and the reaction is less complicated.

It seems to me strange that a reaction so obvious should have been elevated into a hall-mark of the value of tragedy. We are frequently assured that the distinction of tragedy is precisely that its final impact is not depressing. It would be more obvious to enquire in what circumstances it can be depressing. What, in fact, may inhibit the reaction. The answer, I suppose, is that any failure of conviction about the experience of disaster will leave us uneasy; any suspicion that the tragedy was bogus will make our reaction bogus too; it may also be true that if what we have witnessed is not clear, if our dominant sense is of bewilderment, then the reaction will equally lack clarity. It is the business of a tragedy, of the play itself, to be depressing; if in the end it is really encouraging, the sense of disaster will be contained, and the demands on our feelings less acute. In fact, the reassurances of Fortinbras and his like strike us at once as perfunctory; they are not in tune with the tragic experience, and they leave us unaffected.

Consolation Rejected

The relevance of this speculative rumination to *King Lear* is that the process of the play seems to me calculated to repudiate every source of consolation with which we might greet the final disaster. Not even the most perfunctory of reassurances is uttered after Lear has died, and we must assent to Kent's words:

> O! let him pass; he hates him
> That would upon the rack of this tough world
> Stretch him out longer. (V. iii. 313-15)

If that is our final sense of the play, we cannot honestly point to anything that has gone before it as a source of comfort.

This is the reason why, in the last two chapters, a heavy stress has been laid on the continual repudiation of comforting ideas. Many, perhaps most, interpretations of the play since Bradley have found in it some affirmation of faith in life that shines all the brighter for the general darkness. Such affirmations are there, in plenty: 'The worst returns to laughter'; 'This shows you are above, You justicers'; 'Ripeness is all'; 'The Gods are just'; 'All friends shall taste The wages of their virtue'. Subtler than any of these, and much more persuasive, is what Bradley designated the 'redemption' of King Lear, the exchange of contrition and forgiveness with Cordelia which has been claimed as evidence that this is a Christian play. Not that it can be reasonably suggested that this is an explicitly Christian passage: that is to say, there are no direct references to the Christian doctrines it may seem to affirm. But that the pattern of experience represented there is closely related to Christian doctrine is certainly true; and it can be supported by occasional allusions in the text to phrases of the New Testament.

But reflection will hardly allow us to see these ideas as consolations for the play's ending. Firstly, because it is only reflection that brings them back to mind; nothing is said as Lear dies to remind us of them, and it would surely seem impertinent if anything were. Secondly, if we are looking among them for an idea to clutch on to, we shall have to be highly selective. 'Ripeness is all' and 'The Gods are just' are phrases of equal force in the play, and they are from the same speaker; nothing, except personal preference, can encourage us to remember one more favourably than the other. Similarly, if we wish to recall the vividness of New Testament love in Cordelia, we should in honesty recall the equally vivid Old Testament vengeance of Edgar's gods; both at once can be heard in Lear's words as he contemplates life in prison after the battle is lost.

The third reflection which most effectively precludes our treating these phrases as touchstones for our comfort, is the dramatic process in which they are involved. The last two Acts of the play, I have suggested, are constructed of a series of advances and repudiations of visions of hope. Each concept is followed by a scene of intense experience to which the idea cannot be applied. Edgar sees his blinded father immediately after claiming that the worst returns to laughter, and learns that 'the worst is not So long as we can say "this is the worst" '. This is a dialectical pattern, of exchange between theory and experience, which is continually repeated. Gloucester's stoic resolution to abjure suicide is followed by sight of Lear too mad for any moral choice. 'Ripeness is all' leads to 'We two will sing like birds i' th' cage', where no ripeness is possible. The last repetition of this pattern is as simple as the first, when Albany's assertion of poetic justice is met by 'And my poor fool is hang'd! No, no, no life!'

One cannot avoid the conclusion that a pattern thus repeated in subtler or cruder forms is essential to the sense of the play. On the larger scale, the reconciliation of Lear and Cordelia that concludes Act IV, and seems finally to endorse the movement towards relief, is met by the whole experience of Act V. It is the unredeemed Lear who boasts of killing Cordelia's executioner; and the excitement of his words must make us pause before wishing that the redemption had been more lasting. It was, in fact, in large part composed of exhaustion; and it ceases to attract, much as 'justice' becomes repulsive.

The structural process of Acts IV and V is of course involved in the larger mass of the play. Act I began in the confident richness of the royal pageant; the contrary implications of the solitary Edmund, and the melancholic Fool proceed through the stripping of Act II to Lear's discovery of his own nakedness, 'Man's life is cheap as beast's'. Act III makes even that seem cheerful; man, exposed like a beast, suffers most i' th' mind. The 'clothing' that is removed in the first part of the play is that of traditional assurances of position, home and family; it is replaced in Act IV by a clothing of ideas, of justice and redemption. When that too is stripped in Act V, we are left alone with exhaustion and the relief of death. The concepts fade away, but the naked experience remains.

Allegory and Experience

In fact, we may well be moved to feel that the experience is the more vivid because the moral ideas have disappeared. This raises a question about the relation of morality to dramatic experience in the play. I called attention in the prologue to the implausibility of the 'plot' abstracted from the play. And in reviewing the structure I often used terms more suggestive of moral allegory than of a compulsive sequence of events. Yet it cannot be doubted that the ultimate quality in the play is the depth of its living experience. It is thus at once the nearest of Shakespeare's plays to allegory, and the furthest from it. Much of the play is very obviously allegorical: Edgar and Gloucester in the last two Acts are the clearest instance. With them, the moral demonstration continually exceeds the dramatic experience, or at least is disproportionately obtrusive. If the whole play were at that level, we might be interested, but we could not be profoundly moved. Yet Lear's scenes are not so widely different: Lear waking in Cordelia's arms, or Cordelia dead in Lear's arms likewise have allegorical significance (I have remarked how often the stage picture is emblematic). The difference between these two is not fortuitous: Edgar's morality play is exposed by Lear's experience; or by contrary, we are assured of the naturalness of Lear's experience partly by feeling its contrast with the demonstrative allegory applied to Gloucester. The sense of 'naturalness' in drama is always partly relative; if one scene is more natural than its predecessor, we may easily come to feel that it is absolutely natural.

The allegorical sets off the natural; but it also carries it. It is the sequence of moral discoveries which is coherent in the play, rather than the dramatic events. At each significant moment, the human experience is supremely vivid; but the links between them are not essentially narrative in kind. This reposes an exceptional weight on the quality of speech that must affirm reality when the plot will hardly suggest it. To this condition I called attention in the prologue, and the quotations in my text should sufficiently attest it. Here again, the contrast between the smooth rhythms of Edgar's scenes and the far more varied and flexible utterances of Lear is conspicuous.

The final sense is that all moral structures, whether of natural order

conc

or Christian redemption, are invalidated by the naked fact of experience. The dramatic force of this rests on the human impulse to discover a pattern, a significance, by investigating nature. But nature itself finally frustrates that impulse; when Lear dies, the moral voices are silenced. We are left with unaccommodated man indeed; naked, unsheltered by any consolation whatsoever. This, one may say, is the function of all tragedy. But it is not a purely aesthetic function; the artistic impulse is to complete a pattern, which is to affirm an aesthetic order, whether its moral equivalent is apparent or not. This, too, *Lear* directly resists: again and again during the last Act we seem to approach the completion of a pattern which might transcend disaster; but each coda is broken off by a renewed sense of its inadequacy, and so again we are left to Lear's deluded death without even the aesthetic consolation of formal patterning.

Superfluity

We are, in short, forced by the remorseless process of *King Lear* to face the fact of its ending without any support from systems of moral or artistic belief at all.[1] It is the most painful thing in our, perhaps in any, literature. That is what makes it supreme, even among tragedies. The resurgence of feeling as we leave the theatre is free of uncertainty, because the fact has really been faced. Nature has no moral order; and we can no longer wish for one. Cordelia dies, and Lear retreats into insanity. It would be naïve to call this pessimistic, when any effort at optimism would be patently false, and therefore more 'depressing'. Evil is all-embracing and finally destructive; but it co-exists with its unequal opposite: affection, kindness, love. Nature has no 'need' of either; and, being superfluous, they cannot be measured against each other. The best we can do is to accept that superfluity. Our feelings, crushed by facing ultimate negation, are simultaneously channelled towards recognising the perpetual vitality of the most vulnerable virtues. Large orders collapse; but values remain, and are independent of them.

[1] I have analysed this structural process more fully in "The Ending of *King Lear*", *Shakespeare 1564-1964*, ed. E. A. Bloom, 1964.

APPENDIX

Date and Text

King Lear was entered in the Stationers' Register (as a preliminary to publication) on 26 November 1607. The entry describes it 'as yt was played before the kings maiestie . . . vppon St Stephans night at Christmas Last'. It certainly existed, then, by 26 December 1606; but it had probably been played in the public theatre before that. There is no doubt that Shakespeare made use, in writing his play, of the old play, *King Leir*, which was printed in 1605. This would seem to give fairly secure grounds for dating *King Lear* 1605–6.

However, there are doubts. W. W. Greg called attention to the possibility that the old play had been printed in 1605, not at random, but in order to cash in on the success of Shakespeare's new play. He pointed to its entry in the Stationers' Register, where the word 'Tragedie' has been crossed out, and 'Tragecall historie' substituted. Since the old play has a happy ending, it may seem odd that 'Tragedie' should ever have been written (not very odd: tragi-comedies like *Cymbeline* were described as tragedies; besides, the narrative versions of the story were all tragic). Further, the title page advertises the play 'as it hath bene diuers and sundry times lately acted'. Because it is so obviously antiquated, this seems improbable, and may really refer to Shakespeare's play (again, such an advertisement might have been made in any case). These points are not individually very strong, but together they do support a natural suspicion about the sudden decision to print a long-forgotten play.

If that were so, *King Lear* must be dated before 8 May 1605, when *King Leir* was entered in the register. The problem then is, how did Shakespeare come to make use of the old play? Details of plot he might have recalled from seeing it many years before; but verbal echoes would rather suggest that he read a manuscript in the theatre's possession. Other evidences for an earlier date are weightless. Professor Muir finds it unlikely that Shakespeare wrote *Macbeth* (1606) and *Lear* in the same year. On the other hand, the resemblances I have commented on between *Lear* and Shakespeare's last plays, as well as its well-known likeness to

Timon of Athens, would tend to support a later date. The simplest treatment of the evidence would lead us to accept 1605-6, but the suspicion remains that it might have been written as early as 1604. It is generally accepted that *Lear* was written before *Macbeth*, though even that is not certain.

The first edition of the play, in quarto size, appeared in 1608 (a second quarto, also dated 1608, was in fact a copy of the first, printed in 1619 with a forged title page, because of copyright trouble). The second edition was in the 1623 Folio of all Shakespeare's plays. The two are broadly similar, though with frequent minor disagreements; the Folio omits some 300 lines which are in the Quarto, and adds another 100 which the earlier text is lacking. The printer of the Folio seems to have used a copy of the Quarto which had been corrected after comparison with a manuscript. Although the Quarto text is generally fairly sound, it persistently deranges the verse lines, and sometimes ascribes passages to the wrong speaker. It is generally assumed to have been printed from a manuscript which had been composed by ear, either from memory (an exceptionally good memory, not impossible for an actor), or, rather carelessly, from dictation. Its omissions seem to be the result of carelessness. The manuscript used in preparing the Folio copy seems to have been the theatre prompt-book; its omissions may probably have been theatre cuts (not necessarily the only cuts made).

The Folio is clearly the more reliable; but both because it does largely depend on the Quarto, and because copying can introduce many errors in fifteen or more years, it is not necessarily better evidence than the earlier text for what Shakespeare wrote; for that may have been dictated from his own manuscript, and was in any case produced much nearer in time to the writing of the play. All modern editions are composed of a mixture of both, varying only in how frequently the editor feels a decided preference for a Quarto reading. One passage, III. ii. 79-96, which appears only in the later text, used to be thought of as an interpolation by another author. It is now generally accepted as authentic, though the New Cambridge Edition proposes a rearrangement which makes it more intelligible.

Further Reading

Critical Editions

The Arden Shakespeare, ed. Kenneth Muir (1952)

The New Shakespeare, ed. G. I. Duthie and J. Dover Wilson (Cambridge 1960)

(Paperback editions are also available in the New Penguin and Signet Shakespeare)

Earlier Criticism

S. Johnson, notes in his edition of Shakespeare. See *Johnson on Shakespeare*, ed. W. Raleigh (1925)

C. Lamb, 'On the Tragedies of Shakespeare, considered with reference to their fitness for stage representation.' In *Lamb's Criticism*, ed. E. M. W. Tillyard (1923)

S. T. Coleridge, *Shakespeare Criticism*, ed. T. M. Raysor

A. C. Bradley, *Shakespearean Tragedy* (1904)

Recent Criticism

R. B. Heilman, *This Great Stage* (1948)

J. F. Danby, *Shakespeare's Doctrine of Nature* (1949)

Maynard Mack, *King Lear in Our Time* (1966)

W. R. Elton, *King Lear and the Gods* (1966), a study of Renaissance ideas behind the play

Other valuable essays will be found in:

G. Wilson Knight, *The Wheel of Fire* (1930)

D. G. James, *The Dream of Learning* (1951)

L. C. Knights, *Some Shakespearean Themes* (1959) [The essay on *King Lear* was reprinted, with a new conclusion, from *The Pelican Guide to English Literature 2, The Age of Shakespeare* (1955)]

J. Holloway, *The Story of the Night* (1961)

E. A. Bloom (Ed.), *Shakespeare 1564–1964* (1964)

F. Kermode (Ed.), *Shakespeare: King Lear. A Casebook* (1969)

Shakespeare Survey (1960)

Index